Snack Time
Around the World

by **Michele Zurakowski**

illustrated by **Jeff Yesh**

Thanks to our advisers for their
expertise, research, and advice:

JoAnne Buggey, Ph.D., Elementary Social Studies
College of Education and Human Development
University of Minnesota, Minneapolis
Member, National Council for the Social Studies

Susan Kesselring, M.A., Literacy Educator
Rosemount-Apple Valley-Eagan (Minnesota) School District

PICTURE WINDOW BOOKS
Minneapolis, Minnesota

The editor wishes to thank Susanne Mattison, Culinary Specialist for Byerly's,
for her expert advice on preparing the recipes for this book.

Managing Editor: Bob Temple
Creative Director: Terri Foley
Editor: Sara E. Hoffmann
Editorial Adviser: Andrea Cascardi
Copy Editor: Laurie Kahn
Designer: Nathan Gassman
Page production: Picture Window Books
The illustrations in this book were rendered digitally.

Picture Window Books
5115 Excelsior Boulevard
Suite 232
Minneapolis, MN 55416
1-877-845-8392
www.picturewindowbooks.com

To Aidan, Cian, and snack-masters everywhere
—M.Z.

Library of Congress Cataloging-in-Publication Data
Zurakowski, Michele.
Snack time around the world / by Michele Zurakowski ;
illustrated by Jeff Yesh.
p. cm. — (Meals around the world)
Summary: Discusses the variety of foods people around the
world might have for snacks.
ISBN 1-4048-0283-5 (Reinforced Library Binding)
1. Snack foods—Juvenile literature. 2. Cookery, International—
Juvenile literature.
[1. Snack foods. 2. Food habits.] I. Yesh, Jeff, 1971- ill. II. Title.
III. Series.
TX740.Z87 2004
641.5'39—dc22   2003016447

You're hungry. Your tummy is growling so loudly you think there might be a dragon in there. *You need a snack!* Just like you, children all around the world sometimes need snacks to keep going.

NORTH
AMERICA

UNITED STATES
pages 6-7

MEXICO
pages 8-9

SOUTH
AMERICA

What are they eating and drinking?
Let's travel around the world and
find out!

One reason popcorn is so popular is that it's easy to make. People used to pop popcorn in pans on their stoves. Today, most people make popcorn in microwave ovens. Pop! Pop! Pop! Once the popping slows, the snack is ready to eat.

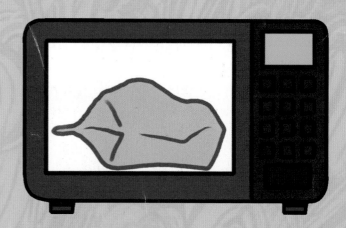

In Mexico, children sometimes eat snacks instead of evening meals. If you had this kind of *merienda* (mer-ee-EN-da), or snack, you might eat some warm sweet rolls and drink a cup of hot chocolate.

Mexican rolls come in all shapes. Munch on a tasty braid, a shell, or a horn. Once you bite through the soft, warm bread, you'll find a surprise. Inside is a mouthful of sweet whipped cream. Dunk your roll in your hot chocolate. Who knew a bedtime snack could be this much fun?

In England, afternoon is the time for a snack. Many people take time to relax and sip cups of tea. Children usually add spoonfuls of sugar and lots of milk to their steaming cups. If they don't like tea, English children might enjoy *smash*, a drink made of fruit juice and water.

Children nibble on treats at teatime. Plates of biscuits or bread-and-butter sandwiches are placed next to the teapot. Some grown-ups eat tiny cakes with their tea. Many children prefer packets of crunchy *crisps* (potato chips).

Australians take time for afternoon tea, too.
But instead of drinking tea, children in Australia like glasses
of milk mixed with strawberry or chocolate flavoring.

Sweet rolls called coffee scrolls are yummy snacks.
Some people get hungry for salty treats, so they grab
bags of cheese- or chicken-flavored puffs.

Cheese Puffs

The markets of Senegal are filled with the wonderful smell of roasting peanuts. Stop at a small shop and buy a bag of peanuts for a noontime snack.

If you have any money left over, walk to another shop. Buy some sugar cookies spread with thick peanut butter. These treats are called *cinq centimes* (sank sahn-TEEM) cookies, which means "five cents." But you probably will have to pay more than that for this delicious snack.

The marketplace in the Philippines also is a good spot to find snacks. If you went to the marketplace with your mom or dad, you could bite into some *lumpia* (LOOM-pee-yah). They look like egg rolls but are lighter and crispier. You also could slurp up some thin noodles called *misua* (MEE-soo-ah). If you still were hungry, you could try a scoop of vanilla ice cream.

In Vietnam, the weather is hot and steamy.
A snack is a good way to cool off. Vietnamese children
enjoy frosty glasses of iced sugarcane juice. Ahhh!

A refreshing drink called *limonada* (lee-mo-NA-da) is a favorite snack in Oman. Make a glass of *limonada* with fresh-squeezed lime or lemon juice, sugar, and fizzy soda water. Careful! The sweet drink can send bubbles up your nose.

Instead of eating in markets or shops, children in Oman eat their snacks at home. They cut up pieces of pita bread and dip them in hummus or tahini. Hummus is a tangy dip made with crushed chickpeas, garlic, and lemon juice. Tahini is a spread made from sesame seeds.

People all around the world like the taste of peanuts and corn. What if you mixed the two tastes together? If you lived in Israel, you might munch on a snack of peanut-flavored puffed corn.

You could wash down your crunchy corn snack with a sweet glass of *mitz* (MEETS). *Mitz* is made from fruit syrup mixed with soda water.

Sometimes three meals a day just don't fill you up. When that happens, children all around the world reach for snacks. Everyone seems to like something sweet, something salty, something crunchy, or something bubbly. What would *you* like for a snack today?

Try These Fun Recipes

You Can Make Pita Bread with Hummus

Makes 2 servings

What you need: 1 piece of pita bread, hummus spread from the store

What to do:

1. Cut pita bread into small, triangular pieces.

2. Spread about one teaspoon (5 ml) of hummus onto each piece of pita bread.

Make sure you have an adult to help you.

You Can Make *Cinq Centimes* Cookies

Makes 12 cookies

What you need:

12 sugar cookies from the store or bakery

12 tablespoons (180 grams) peanut butter (creamy or chunky)

1 cup (240 grams) peanuts

Make sure you have an adult to help you.

What to do:

1. Spread about 1 tablespoon (15 grams) of peanut butter on each cookie. Leave a little bit of space around the edge of the cookie.

2. Chop the peanuts into small pieces.

3. Sprinkle a few peanut pieces on each cookie.

Share the cookies with your friends the way Senegalese children do!

Fun Facts

- The oldest known ears of popping corn were found in a cave in New Mexico. They are believed to be more than 5,000 years old.

- People have been eating chocolate in what is now Mexico for thousands of years. Chocolate is made from cocoa beans. The ancient Mayans used cocoa beans as money!

- In England, the phrase *cup of tea* is so common that people sometimes shorten it to *cuppa*. Someone might say, "I'll have a *cuppa*, please." Everyone in England knows this means you'd like a cup of tea.

- Australian schoolchildren often buy their teatime snacks at the tuckshop. Most schools in Australia have tuckshops. *Tuck* is short for *tucker,* which is an old Australian word for food.

Glossary

chickpea—a type of bean popular in Middle Eastern, Asian, and Latin American cooking

misua—thin noodles eaten in the Philippines

pita bread—a round, flat bread that has an opening like a pocket. You can stuff foods inside it or use it as a scoop.

smash—a drink made of fruit juice and water

tahini—a smooth paste made of sesame seeds

To Learn More

At the Library

Cooper, Elisha. *Ice Cream*. New York: Greenwillow Books, 2002.

Frost, Helen. *Eating Right*. Mankato, Minn.: Pebble Books, 2000.

Landau, Elaine. *Popcorn*. Watertown, Mass.: Charlesbridge Pub., 2003.

Pickering, Robin. *I Like Chocolate*. New York: Children's Press, 2000.

Priceman, Marjorie. *How to Make an Apple Pie and See the World*. New York: Knopf, 1994.

Fact Hound

Fact Hound offers a safe, fun way to find Web sites related to this book. All of the sites on Fact Hound have been researched by our staff.

http://www.facthound.com

1. Visit the Fact Hound home page.
2. Enter a search word related to this book, or type in this special code: 1404802835.
3. Click on the FETCH IT button.

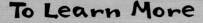

Your trusty Fact Hound will fetch the best sites for you!

Index